Mini Quilts

by Anita Murphy & her friends

Additional ASN Books by Anita Murphy:
Drunkard's Path, An Easy No-Pins Technique, ASN #4128
Reversible Quilts, An Easy New Technique, ASN #4131

Bobbie Matela, Managing Editor
Carol Wilson Mansfield, Art Director
Linda Causee, Editor
Meredith Montross, Associate Editor
Graphic Solutions, Book Design
Fred Huetter, Illustration

Before You Begin

FABRIC

Nothing equals or beats a 100% cotton for quilting, although many different fabrics have a "use me" look. The textures and deeper shades of fabrics other than cotton sometimes just can't be passed up. In making the mini quilts in this book, fabric needs will be very minimal. The fabrics and colors used will be the result of which doll bed or wall space is being used. If your mini quilt will be displayed on an antique doll bed, keep in mind that after completing the small quilt, a tea or dye bath can give it that look of yesteryear.

Throughout this book, the fabric requirements with each pattern allow for a little extra fabric — not enough to hurt, but enough to help. Remember, what's left over will fit nicely in a labeled shoe box for your next project!

BUYING FABRIC

Always try to buy a little extra when buying fabric. So often, when you use a certain fabric, its placement along side another fabric makes you want to try a different quilt design. If your new design requires more fabric than your originally planned design, the sadness in not having enough fabric on hand is equal to a dark and rainy day.

Several years ago, while teaching and judging in Iowa, I was invited to sit in on a Guild meeting where members discussed how they organized their fabrics. One dear lady said that she had purchased two under-the-bed-size plastic boxes. As she cut out a garment or had a small amount of fabric left from planning a large size quilt, she cut leftover fabric into squares using a 4" or 6" plastic template. She then placed the cut squares in the boxes. She further related that when she could not sleep as late as the rest of her family, she could slide out her 4" or 6" box and not have to go through shelves of fabric to find what she needed for a scrap quilt. I have since started my two boxes, and enjoy going through them when I have a special color need. It sure saves pulling out yards of fabric and then having to refold it.

After finishing some of the mini quilts in this book, you may want to start a box labeled 1", 2" or even 3" cuts of fabric! I have a shoe box full of 1 1/2" cut strips and I am pleased as punch at how handy they are.

WHAT IS A FAT QUARTER?

Knowing that not everyone has been collecting fabrics for several years, and knowing the need to add just one more color to a project, I have used fat quarters in several of the yardage requirements throughout this book. A fat quarter,

Fig 1, is a quarter of a yard of fabric that is cut in such a way that you can get 18" cuts on the lengthwise grain. Quilt shops often have rolled up baskets of fat quarters arranged in attractive color assortments. This way, a quilter can quickly add a large range of assorted solid and prints to their projects as well as to their "stash" of fabrics.

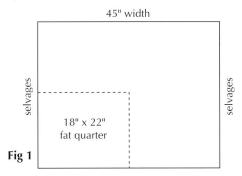

QUILT SIZES

The purpose of this book is to share some easy techniques for mini wall hangings and doll bed quilts. There is no set rule for making mini quilts, so let the child within you come out. Make something just for the fun of it or to see that wonderful smile on a child's face when you give them a new quilt for their favorite doll or teddy bear. The quilts in this book range from 6" x 6" for a doll house quilt to 23" x 23" for a wall quilt.

CUT OR TEAR FABRIC

Many people think that by tearing fabric they are getting a straight edge. Not so! When the fabric is washed, the crooked edge will reappear. I cannot help but note the long strips of thrown away fabric when quilters straighten torn fabric to get rid of the little "whiskers" on the torn edges. So ask to have your fabric cut rather than torn.

TO WASH OR NOT TO WASH

Throughout this book, only small amounts of fabrics will be needed to complete a project. Therefore, instead of using a washing machine, just dip your fabric in the basin and iron them wet on a white terry cloth towel. If you do not see any color bleeding, press and set aside to use later.

ODORS

Some fabrics have a chemical smell from the dye process and some fabrics absorb odors such as cigarette smoke. Washing with a bit of soap will usually remove an odor, but if it continues to linger, do not put the fabric in with your other fabrics because soon it will share its odor with the rest of your collection. First, place the fabric in a plastic bag with a new bar of Safeguard™ soap. Tie and seal the bag tightly and leave it for three to four days. I have never had this technique fail even when I used it on ready made clothing. I know we are not supposed to name a certain brand, but I have tried it with many other soaps, and this is the only one I have really had success with. You can use this technique on your finished quilt by using a larger plastic bag.

STRAIGHT OF THE GOODS (Grainline)

Using the straight of the goods or grainline of 100% cotton fabric can't be beat. You will be doing yourself a big favor, especially on the really tiny pieces you will be cutting and stitching, if you cut on the straight of the goods. Your work will lie flatter and look so much neater. Even bindings will behave better when cut on the straight of the goods.

SUPPLIES: B.Y.O.S.B.
(Bring Your Own Sewing Basket)

Whether you are working at home, teaching a workshop, going to a workshop, or helping with a hands-on project at a Guild meeting, nothing beats having good working tools. You can find lots of "goodies" in an office supply store to include in your sewing basket such as template plastic, rulers, tracing paper, pencils, pencil sharpener and permanent marking pens (such as the Pilot SC-UF pen). Other supplies can be found at your local quilt or fabric shop.

Scissors: You must have a family pair — you know the ones in the kitchen drawer, that can be used to cut roses, wire, plastic tags off clothing, etc. Next, you will need a better scissors that will cut template plastic, construction paper, etc. Finally, you must have a pair of good fabric scissors that will cut from six to eight layers of fabric at once. These are the scissors that you must keep hidden where no one else will find and use them.

Rotary cutter and mat: For many projects, these are a real must. When using a rotary cutter, the special mat designed for it needs to be used. A handy tip for keeping your mat clean is to rub nylon net over the scratches; this removes the bits of fabric that get embedded in the mat. Another hint for keeping your mat in prime condition is to always keep it flat, especially when transporting it in a hot car. If the mat does get warped, try laying it flat outside in full sunlight.

Seam ripper: This is a useful tool to have when those little gremlins make your seams skip or go crooked and you have to do some reverse stitching.

Rulers: They come in all sizes, widths and lengths, but buy one thick enough to use both for marking and rotary cutting. A word of advice, wipe the edge of your ruler after every project. It can get awfully soiled and sure to shootin' that soil will rub off on a light piece of fabric.

Ironing board and iron: Due to the small size of the projects in this book, you will find that many patterns need to be pressed with every row stitched. So make a small elbow ironing board by covering the cardboard that fabric comes wrapped on with fleece or heavy fabric, or both. You can keep it right next to your sewing machine and you won't have to get up as often. If you scorch a fabric, soak it for 20 minutes in hydrogen peroxide.

Needles, hand and machine: As the old adage says, you usually get what you pay for. So spend the little extra and invest in good quality sewing machine needles and hand sewing needles. I find that a #10 needle is best for hand sewing. If you have trouble threading your needle, turn it over. Since the eye of a needle is punched out, one side of the eye is larger than the other making it easier to thread. Also, by cutting your thread at an angle, it will slide right in without a miss.

Pencils and sharpener: Sharpen your soft white and silver pencils by hand with an eyeliner sharpener and they won't wear down so fast.

Sewing machine and extra filled bobbins: Be a friend to your sewing machine by keeping it well oiled and clean. I use chicken or bird feathers to clean between the bobbin case and the under side of the throat plate. Having bobbins filled ahead of time for each project, helps your work go more smoothly.

Thread: As with so many quilters' items, purchase the best. If you value your investment of good fabric and time, purchase 100% cotton thread or the best poly-wrapped cotton thread available.

Some of the mini quilts in this book are quilted with wonderful metallic threads adding a bit of soft luster to the overall effect. When machine quilting, use a good quality mono-filament thread on top of the machine and a regular matching thread on the bobbin. (Do remember that quilting thread is only to be used for hand quilting.)

When hand sewing, a helpful hint is to thread your needle before actually cutting the thread. That way you will be sewing in the direction that the manufacturer stretched it onto the spool eliminating knots and tangles.

Pins: Use a very thin pin with a beaded head. They are easier to see and pull from your fabric as you are stitching. Pins with too large a shank tend to displace your fabric pieces as you pin them. Put aside those large pins and use them the next time you need to hang a small picture on the wall.

Pincushions: I suggest having two pincushions, one on your cutting table and one next to your sewing machine. After you empty the one on your cutting table and fill the one next to your sewing machine, exchange them. This will help to eliminate pins on the floor to be found by someone's bare foot.

(continued)

Remember to place your needles in that little strawberry on the top of the pincushion. It is full of graphite and will help to keep your needle sharp.

Another helpful hint is to place a leftover square of fleece (about 12" x 12") next to your sewing machine. Snipped threads and bits of cut fabrics attach themselves to the fleece and you don't have all that "trash" to pick up off the floor. When you have finished sewing, it is very easy to pick up the strings and snippets, toss them in the waste basket, and put your fleece back down on the table.

WORK PLACE
Even when working with mini quilts, a designated work place is necessary. You need a place to cut, a place to sew and a place to pin up your quilt blocks, such as a felt board or a wall.

STORAGE OR STASHING FABRICS
The plastic organizers with snap tight lids are perfect for storing fabrics. They are the right height to slide under your bed and you can see through them to identify the fabrics at a glance. We all need separate containers for cottons, silks, wools, velvets, laces, etc. Most of the fabrics used for the quilts in this book used to live in shoe boxes. They are so easy to tuck in and under and behind the towels and sheets in the hall and bathroom closets.

CUTTING
When cutting fabric, I can't emphasize enough the importance of cutting your fabric with thought to the future. For example, if the fabric may be used for a border or binding, cut it where you will be leaving the full length intact. This ensures that you will not find at the last moment that your borders or bindings need to be pieced. The best method to achieve this is to follow the sample cutting diagram in **Fig 2**. Plan the number of squares and/or triangles you are going to need, then cut them toward one side of the fabric. Use the balance of the fabric for your border and binding strips.

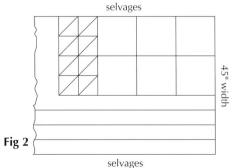

Fig 2

In quilting workshops, teachers are always asked what their favorite method of cutting is. The answer is to cut the way you are most comfortable. Practice always helps, but start out slowly and let your hand warm up a bit. After all,

even the runners at the 26-mile marathon warm up at the beginning of a race. Always remember that good sharp tools are a real plus.

A little tip is to stack your fabric pieces alternately as you cut them. For example, when cutting triangles from six layers of fabric at a time, turn every six triangles in the opposite direction as you stack them, **Fig 3**. You will be able to count your cuts more quickly and will be able to pick up each group by the corner in multiples of six.

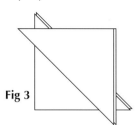

Fig 3

THE SEWING MACHINE
While teaching workshops, I smile within when I hear different students praise the merits of THEIR sewing machines. Yet, many a dear sit there with a fifty or sixty year old featherweight and hum right along with the others. Many of us now have a walking foot that will fit on these little machines giving us an even feed and a 1/4"-wide foot for a guide. Of course, no one can resist longing for one of the new super models that can write, quilt, and do everything but make a cup of tea.

Always remember to tell your machine that you are boss. If you're in control, your machine won't be so apt to frustrate you. If it does, that is the time to stop and fix a hot cup of tea. One of the greatest deeds you can do for your machine is to keep it well oiled and clean. An accumulation of dust and lint in the bobbin case under the throat plate will often be the cause of skipped stitches and breaking threads.

Another good rule to follow, if at all possible, is not to change machines in the middle of a project. Often the 1/4" guideline is a bit different, and at the end of several rows of stitching you will find your work is often 1/4" or more off. It's kind of like the old saying, "Leave the dance with the one you came with."

REVERSE STITCHING
There are some words even in the quilting world that have a grating effect on your ears and thoughts. One such word is RIPPING. It sounds like trouble, so I refer to it as reverse stitching. Yes, there is also reverse quilting, and most of us have done some of that as well. Try to remember: A man or woman would do nothing if they waited until they could do it so well that no one, including themselves, would find fault in what they had done!

It might help to remember my three rules if you are unhappy with your project:

Rule #1: Do reverse stitching (rip it out).

Rule #2: Try to press it out.

Rule #3: Look at it again and decide if you can live with it. If you can't live with it, then try Rule #2. If you still can't live with it then refer back to Rule #1.

A helpful reverse stitching rule that I would like to share with you is to snip about every fifth or sixth stitch of your top thread. Turn your work over and on the back side with an even gentle tug, pull the bottom thread out. Usually one smooth action tug will do the trick. Be cautious that you don't tug or pull too hard because whether you are working on straight of the goods or the bias, you don't want to stretch or distort your fabric.

TEMPLATES

Another item all quilters need is good template material. A great deal of quilting is now accomplished with a ruler, but many quilters still use and need good template material. I would also strongly advise you to invest in a pen that writes on and does not wipe off plastic. Pilot SC-UF and Sakura make the best. Of course, if you need to change any wording, a bit of fingernail polish remover will wipe it clean.

I am often asked if I cut on the line, inside the line or outside the drawn line when tracing templates. The choice is yours, BUT BE CONSISTENT. If you cut the same on all of your template pieces, you will not have a problem. A big favor you can also do for yourself is to always cut out the notches often found on template patterns. They are really there to help you match your pattern pieces.

In making, sharing or creating new templates, always write the following information on the pieces:

1. The size of the finished block

2. If the seam allowance is included in the template

3. Is it the right as well as the left piece?

4. Your initials and the date

STORING TEMPLATES

Where do you keep the template pieces once you have cut them out? Try using a three ring binder, divider sheets, and 7" x 8 3/4" reclosable plastic bags. Place pieces in a bag and staple them to the divider sheets and label them. Catherine Anthony showed this trick to a class many years ago, and it is still one of my most used methods of storing those tiny template pieces. It truly gives you the luxury of always being able to find the size template you need.

PRESSING

Please note that I did not say ironing. Ironing is when you stretch fabric to make it lay flat with no wrinkles. True, you do not want wrinkles in your fabric, but you should always press, NOT iron your fabric. The best hint I can give you to remove wrinkles is to keep a spritz bottle on your ironing board that is half filled with water and half white vinegar. I also recommend drawing the size of your block on a piece of cardboard, then taking that and your newly stitched pieced block to the ironing board. When pressing, see if you are distorting the block by stretching it as you press. It helps to see if you are guilty of over pressing so that you can be more careful in the future.

BATTINGS

What wonderful choices of battings we now have! To decide which batting to use, think about what life style your new project will have. Will it be tied for a special child to take off to college with them? Will it be a doll bed quilt for that dear one who takes her doll with her wherever she goes? Will it be a wall piece? Study the manufacturer's descriptions, and then choose. Most battings now have bonded surfaces and don't need to be quilted less than four inches apart.

When first starting your quilt, take your batting out of the wrapper and let it unwind. It can be a mess when you try to use batting straight out of the package since it is rolled so tight it wants to stay that way. So give it a day or two to unwind. Also, don't try to stretch a smaller square of batting to fit a larger size block. It will eventually shrink back and cause your project to pucker.

MASTER SQUARES

A master square is a square of template plastic used to check that all of your blocks are equal in size. Even for mini quilts, you need to keep your blocks as accurate and as square as possible. If you are hand sewing, make your master square the size of your finished block (no seam allowance) and draw an "X" from corner to corner. If you are machine piecing, make your master square the size of your smallest finished block with seam allowances included and draw an "X" from corner to corner. Place master square on the block and trim to size. It sure helps in joining your blocks, when they are all cut the same size.

PRAIRIE POINTS

Even though you are working with much smaller patterns and blocks when making mini quilts, you can still enjoy the extra spark that prairie points add to any quilt. You will find the only difference is that you will cut the size of your squares 1" or 2" rather than 3" as on a full size quilt.

(continued)

Referring to **Fig 4**, start with a 1" or 2" square; fold in half then fold corners down to meet in middle. Press and pin in place. Pin a row of prairie points, fold side up, along edge of top side of quilt, **Fig 5**. Next, pin another row of prairie points, fold side down, in between previously pinned prairie points, **Fig 6**.

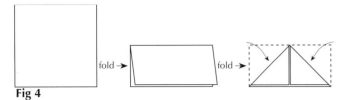

Fig 4

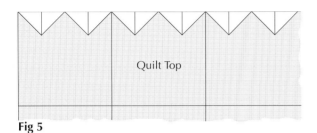

Fig 5

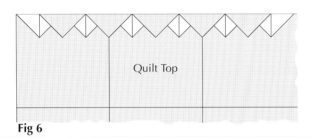

Fig 6

Cut a binding strip of matching fabric 1 1/4" wide by width of quilt where prairie points are being attached. Fold strip in half lengthwise with right side out. **DO NOT PRESS.** When you fold it over, the pressed line never falls where you want it, and you wish you could remove it. So don't press it! Place this strip over the top of prairie points, matching all raw edges, **Fig 7**. Stitch through all layers using a 1/4" seam allowance. Fold your binding over raw edge toward back of quilt and your prairie points stand right up.

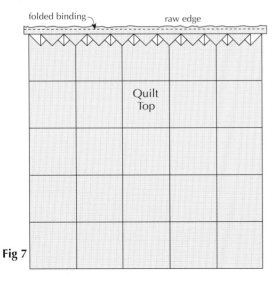

Fig 7

Blind stitch the binding to the back, using caution not to have your stitches go into the front of your quilt where they might be seen.

ROAD MAPS

Just because you are working with smaller pieces and smaller blocks, doesn't mean that in stitching them together you can't get one upside down or turned the wrong way. So please take this hint to heart. You owe it to yourself to have a break after creating all your blocks and pin them up. Step back and look at the blocks from a bit of a distance. I bet you a cup of hot tea, that you will change one or two blocks because the colors seem to fit better another way. Once you have decided on a final placement of your blocks, take small pieces of paper about 2" square. Before you take your blocks down, safety pin the papers on each and every block, marking your blocks Row 1 Block 1, Row 1 Block 2, etc., **Fig 8**. This takes time, but not nearly as much time as having to reverse stitch and restitch a row of blocks.

Fig 8

FINISHING MINI QUILTS

Pillowcase Method 1

Since the life styles of many of these dear, small works of art aren't going to be stressful, many are finished by the old-fashioned method of making a backing to fit the front, then stitching right sides together as in **Fig 9**. Cut a square snip out of the corners before turning it, as in **Fig 10,** and your corners will lay flatter when turned. **A word of caution:** Be careful not to cut your stitched seam! The project is then turned right side out, and sewn closed with invisible stitches.

If you like the look of a binding, you can hand or machine stitch a half inch or less from the edge to give your work a finished look, almost as if it had a binding.

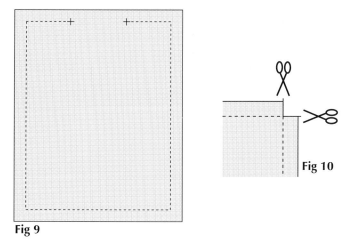

Fig 9

Pillowcase Method 2

Measure the size of your completed quilt top, including borders. Divide lengthwise measurement in half and add 1/2". Cut two backing pieces the crosswise measurement by half the lengthwise measurement plus 1/2".

For example, if your quilt measures 15" x 20", the lengthwise measurement is 20"; divide 20 by 2 which gives 10; add 1/2" to get final measurement of 10 1/2". Cut two pieces of backing fabric 15" x 10 1/2".

Place backing pieces right sides together and stitch a 1/2" seam along the shorter side using long machine basting stitches, **Fig 11**; press seam open.

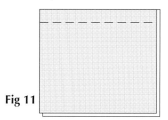

Fig 11

Layer quilt with batting or fleece on bottom, quilt top right side up, then backing right side down. Stitch along all four sides, **Fig 12** (Do not leave an opening); trim corners. Gently remove some of the basting stitches from the backing and turn quilt right side out through opening. Close opening with a blind stitch. Quilt as desired.

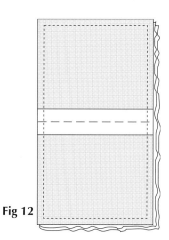

Fig 12

HANGING YOUR MINI QUILTS

A well-attached sleeve will help any size quilt to hang straighter and keep it from sagging. Here are scaled down measurements to create a professional looking sleeve that will fit these smaller treasures.

Take a piece of your backing (or any matching) fabric and cut it 4" wide by the length needed to fit the back of your quilt plus about an inch extra. Fold back 1/4" on each short end and press; stitch in place. Fold each long edge towards middle so that they are touching, not overlapping, **Fig 13**; press firmly. These two pressed creases are very important to the success of attaching your sleeve. Take your two long raw edges and sew them wrong sides together using a 1/2" seam, **Fig 14**. Pin sleeve seamed side down to quilt back (check to be sure it is the top of your wall quilt). Using a hand blind stitch and caution not to have your stitches go clear through to the front, stitch along both creased edges. The sleeve will have a slight bulge, **Fig 15**, but that is where your rod will slide in and give a nice, flat look to the front of the quilt without pulling or puckering.

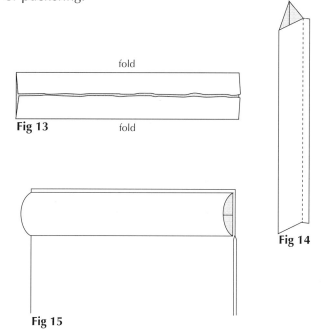

fold

Fig 13   fold

Fig 14

Fig 15

7

Miniature (Dietetic) Biscuits

Shown in color on page 21

APPROXIMATE SIZE: 4 1/2" x 5 1/2"

In the quilt collection at the Smithsonian, there is a beautiful "Puff" or "Grandmother's Biscuit" quilt made some 100 years ago by a 12-year-old boy. He had broken both legs so his mother showed him how to make these dear puffs. While his quilt contains over 1,400 individual silk puffs, this miniature biscuit quilt contains twenty 1"-square "puffs" that were sewn together using my easy technique of stitching the puffs onto a strip of muslin.

FABRIC REQUIREMENTS:

fat quarter pastel print
fat quarter muslin
assorted scraps pastel prints
small amount polyester fiberfill

TEMPLATES:

A 1 1/2" square
B 2" square

CUTTING REQUIREMENTS:

twenty 2" squares from assorted pastel prints
four 2" x 7 1/2" strips from muslin for base
one 5 1/2" x 6 1/2" piece from pastel print for backing

INSTRUCTIONS:

Pin 1/2" pleats on three sides of a pastel square, **Fig 1**. Each pleated side will measure 1 1/2". Repeat for all twenty squares.

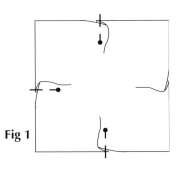

Fig 1

8

Pin five pleated squares right side up on muslin strip with unpleated side on the right, **Fig 2**. Repeat for remaining strips and puffs.

Stitch each row in a continuous line 1/4" from raw edge of puffs, **Fig 3**. Stitching in this manner will leave one end open for stuffing.

Stuff each puff with a pinch of fiberfill — not too full, but enough to stretch out the pleats. Pin pleat on open edge of each puff; stitch, **Fig 5**. Repeat with remaining three strips.

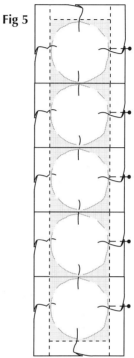

Fig 2   Fig 3

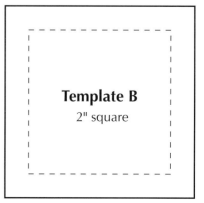

Fig 5

Place strips right sides together; join. Place top, right side up, centered on wrong side of backing. (There should be 1/2" of backing fabric extending around quilt top.) For binding fold backing towards front; blind stitch in place.

To make seams between puffs, take one puff strip and fold first puff right side down over second puff. Stitch just inside previous stitching line so that continuous stitching doesn't show on front side, **Fig 4**. Continue stitching seams between puffs in same manner for rest of strip. Repeat for remaining three strips.

Template A
1 1/2" square

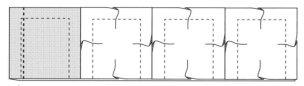

Fig 4

Template B
2" square

Cross-Pieced Miniature Bow Tie

Shown in color on back cover

APPROXIMATE SIZE: 14 1/2" x 17 1/2"

Bow Tie has been a favorite with quilters for many years, and yes, in many sizes. This quilt was made using an easy technique that eliminates the stumbling block of setting in the center square. Enjoy this new method for this old favorite.

FABRIC REQUIREMENTS:

one fat quarter muslin
twenty assorted fabric scraps
1/2 yd dk print for border and backing
one fat quarter bright print for inside border
one 16" x 19" piece of batting or fleece

TEMPLATES:

A bow tie
B triangle
C square

CUTTING REQUIREMENTS:

forty Template A bow ties from muslin
forty Template B triangles from assorted prints
forty Template C squares from same print as B
two 1 1/4" x 13" strips from bright print for inner border
two 1 1/4" x 16" strips from bright print for inner border
two 1 3/4" x 16" strips from dk print for outer border
two 1 3/4" x 15 1/2" strips from dk print for outer border
one 16" x 19" piece from dk print for backing

10

INSTRUCTIONS:

Note: Use same print fabric within each block.

Stitch Template B triangle to Template A bow tie being careful to match the notches. Join this unit to Template C square (from same print fabric as B triangle) making sure the printed fabrics are next to each other as in **Fig 1**. Repeat using same print. Join the two units, turning one in the opposite direction, **Fig 2**. You will need a total of twenty Bow Tie Blocks.

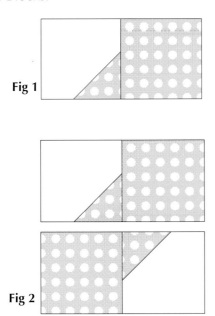

Fig 1

Fig 2

Using Master Square (page 5), square up all of your blocks; arrange blocks as in layout placing the colors to their best advantage. Attach road maps (page 6) and join blocks. Add bright inner border, sides first, then top and bottom. Add outer border in same manner. Using Pillowcase Method 1 (page 6), add backing and quilt either by hand or machine.

Bow Tie Block

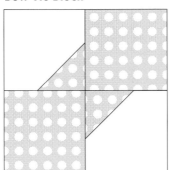

Layout

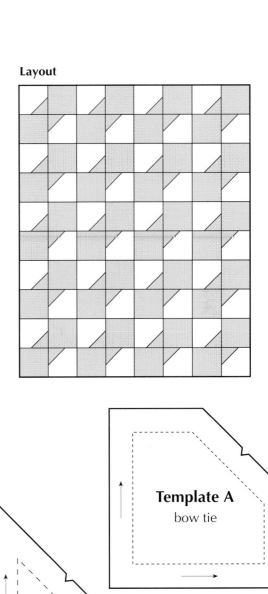

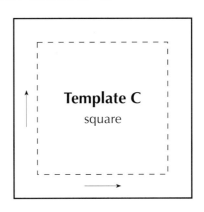

Template A
bow tie

Template B
triangle

Template C
square

11

Hearts of My Heart

Shown in color on page 22

APPROXIMATE SIZE: 22" x 22"

When Isabel Johann married Peter some 33 years ago, she learned to become a high wire performer with the Shrine Circus. Their life with the circus took them to Europe, Australia, Mexico, and Canada, and continues to be a big part of their life as they have two large well-trained elephants. Isabel, however, states that she began quilting in 1983 and it opened the door for new happiness and order to her life. The result of one of her classes with Mary Ellen Hopkins in 1991 is what she is sharing with us in her *Hearts of My Heart*.

The original design and technique for this quilt appears in *Connecting Up* and *Continuing On* by Mary Ellen Hopkins, published by ME Publications. Permission for its use has been granted by Mary Ellen Hopkins.

FABRIC REQUIREMENTS:

1 yd dark print
1/2 yd light print
1/4 yd red/white print (Color 1)
1/4 yd red/blue/yellow print (Color 2)
1/4 yd purple print (Color 3)
1 yd backing fabric
3/4 yd contrasting color for binding
1 yd batting

TEMPLATES:

A side triangle
B corner triangle

CUTTING REQUIREMENTS:

Lattice Blocks

six 1 1/4" x 45" strips from dark print
six 1" x 45" strips from light print

Heart Blocks

one 1 3/4" x 45" strip from Color 1 for hearts
two 1 3/4" x 45" strips from Color 2 for hearts
one 1 3/4" x 45" strip from Color 3 for hearts
two 1 1/4" x 45" strips from dark print
five 7/8" x 45" strips from dark print

Setting Triangles

twenty-four side triangles from dark print
four corner triangles from dark print

INSTRUCTIONS:

LATTICE BLOCKS (make 45)

Sew a dark print strip to each lengthwise edge of three light print strips; press. Cut crosswise at 1 1/4" intervals, **Fig 1**. You will need 90 pieced strips.

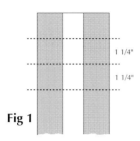

Fig 1

Place pieced strip right side down on light background strip, **Fig 2**; stitch. Continue sewing pieced strips onto light strip, **Fig 3**. Trim light strip between pieced strips, **Fig 4**; press. Chain piece the pieced strips to other side of light background strips, **Fig 5**.

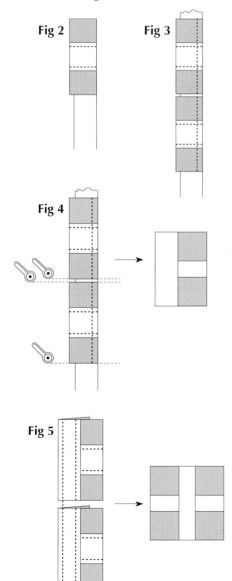

HEART BLOCKS (make 40)

Cut 1 3/4" strips into 2 1/2" lengths (A) and 1 1/4" lengths (B) from each heart color as follows:

eight from Color 1

twenty from Color 2

twelve from Color 3

Cut 7/8" strips into 160 squares (C).

Cut 1 1/4" dark print strips into forty squares (D).

Place the 7/8" squares (C) right sides together on the right and the left upper corners of both the long and short heart fabrics; stitch down from point to point diagonally across the small squares, **Fig 6**; press open. Do not cut away fabric as it helps to stabilize your work.

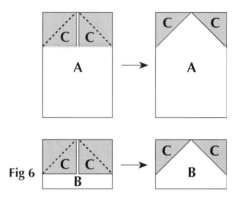

Fig 6

Following **Fig 7**, attach 1 1/4" dark square (D) to the side of short heart piece;

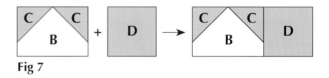

Fig 7

then sew to long heart piece, **Fig 8**. **Note:** These can be chain pieced to speed up your sewing time.

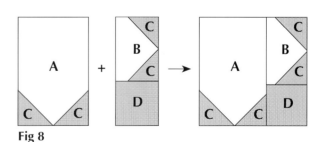

Fig 8

13

(continued)

FINISHING

Join heart and lattice blocks in diagonal rows adding side and corner triangles as needed, **Fig 9**.

Layer quilt with backing wrong side up, then batting and quilt top right side up. Quilt and bind as desired.

Fig 9

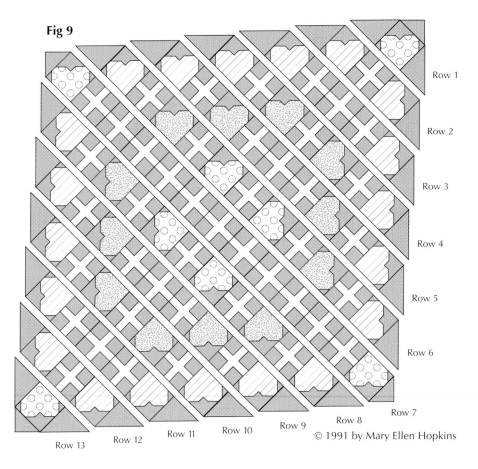

Row 1
Row 2
Row 3
Row 4
Row 5
Row 6
Row 7
Row 8
Row 9
Row 10
Row 11
Row 12
Row 13

© 1991 by Mary Ellen Hopkins

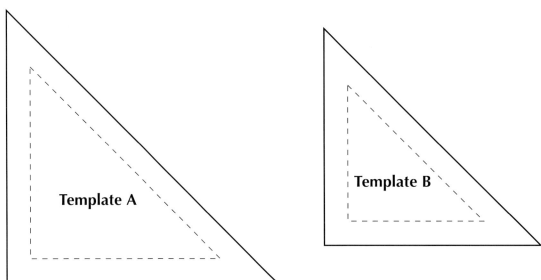

Template A

Template B

14

Sunbonnet Sue in Miniature

Shown in color on back cover

INSTRUCTIONS:

Leaving at least 5/8" on all four sides, mark a grid (3 squares by 3 squares) on one piece of white or muslin fabric. Horizontal lines are spaced 1 1/2" apart and vertical lines, 1 3/8" apart.

Place Sunbonnet Sue template on fabric and turn template until you find a spot where Sue's hat is a different color than her dress. Mark Sue's shape as well as the outside square. Repeat for a total of six Sues facing right; flip template over and mark three Sues facing left. Cut out SQUARES. Following manufacturer's directions, press fusible web to back of Sunbonnet Sue squares. Cut out Sue shapes, peel off paper backing and position in center of each grid square. Press Sue shapes in place following manufacturer's directions.

With one strand of embroidery floss, work buttonhole stitch around her dress, outline stitch for hat, and straight stitches for foot and arm, **Fig 1**.

Pin ribbon pieces over grid lines; stitch in place.

Using Pillowcase Method 1 (page 6) attach backing and batting. Quilt around each square.

APPROXIMATE SIZE: 5" x 5 1/4"

In May of 1980, Gretchen Miertschin was the guest speaker at the Houston Area Quilt Guild Meeting. She showed us how to make an appliqued name tag using a miniature Sunbonnet Sue pattern. I have since enjoyed making mini quilts turning my Sunbonnet Sue template on different print fabrics so that her bonnet is a different color than her dress. A few simple embroidery stitches add the finishing touches.

FABRIC REQUIREMENTS:
one fat quarter of white or muslin
assorted print fabric scraps
small piece of batting or fleece

ADDITIONAL MATERIALS:
1/8 yd paper-backed fusible web
    (i.e. Wonder-Under™)
1 1/4 yds 1/4"-wide satin ribbon
black embroidery floss

TEMPLATES:
Sunbonnet Sue Window Template

CUTTING REQUIREMENTS:
two 5 3/4" high x 5 1/2" wide pieces from white or
    muslin
one 5 3/4" x 5 1/2" piece of batting or fleece
eight 5" lengths of ribbon

**Sunbonnet Sue
Window Template**

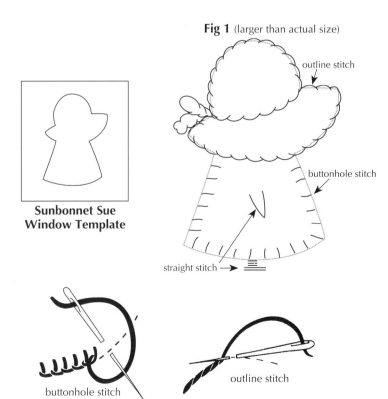

Fig 1 (larger than actual size)

outline stitch

buttonhole stitch

straight stitch →

buttonhole stitch

outline stitch

Boxed Roses

Shown in color on front cover

APPROXIMATE SIZE: 23 1/2" x 23 1/2"

Boxed Roses is a beautiful wall quilt made by Irma Gail Hatcher. She donated this mini quilt to the Celebrity Quilter's Auction at the 1991 Quilt Festival in Houston, and it was the quilt that sold for the most money. Boxed Roses is a miniature quilt made with 16 ruched flowers appliqued to miniature "Jack in the Box" blocks. It has 283 pieces cut from 30 different fabrics, and is machine pieced, hand appliqued and hand quilted. Quick pieced triangles make up the leaves. Thanks again Irma Gail for sharing such a beauty with all of us.

FABRIC REQUIREMENTS:

3/4 yd green print (model has 21 different green scraps)
1/2 yd white
1/2 yd bcigc print
1/2 yd red print (model has 16 different prints -
 each rose requires a 1" x 16" strip)
1 yd large floral print
3/4 yd backing fabric
28" x 28" piece of batting

TEMPLATES:

A rectangle
B rectangle
C triangle
D corner
E square

CUTTING REQUIREMENTS:

fifty-six 2" x 2" squares from green print
forty 2" x 2" squares from white
sixteen 2" x 2" squares from beige
five Template A rectangles from green print
fourteen Template B rectangles from green print
eight Template C triangles from white
four Template D pieces from beige*
four Template D reversed pieces from beige*
four Template E squares from white
sixteen l" x 16" strips from red print or
 assorted red prints
four 3 3/4" x 28" strips from large floral print
*Note: Transfer the dot marking onto each Template D
 piece.

INSTRUCTIONS:

Mark diagonal line on each 2" green print square. Place a 2" green print square right sides together with a 2" white square; stitch 1/4" from each side of diagonal line, **Fig 1**. Repeat until you have forty stitched pairs of squares. Place 2" beige square right sides together with sixteen remaining 2" green squares and stitch in same manner. Cut squares along drawn diagonal line, **Fig 2**. You will have 80 green and white pieced squares and 32 green and beige pieced squares.

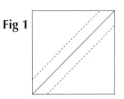
Fig 1

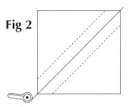
Fig 2

Referring to **Fig 3**, make 28 units in four different arrangements: eight Unit A, eight Unit B, eight Unit C and four Unit D.

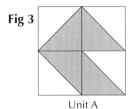
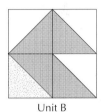

Fig 3

Unit A   Unit B

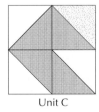
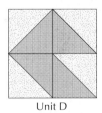

Unit C   Unit D

Join a Unit B and a Unit A to each side of a Template B rectangle for Section 1, **Fig 4**. Repeat three more times.

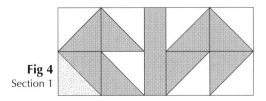

Fig 4
Section 1

Join a Unit D and a Unit C to each side of a Template B rectangle for Section 2, **Fig 5**. Repeat three more times.

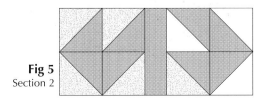

Fig 5
Section 2

(continued)

Join Section 1 and Section 2 to each side of a Template A rectangle to complete Block 1, **Fig 6**. Repeat three more times.

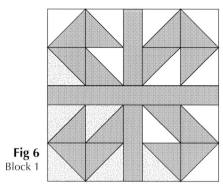

Fig 6
Block 1

Join a Unit A to each side of a Template B rectangle; repeat. Join both Sections to a Template A rectangle to complete Block 2, **Fig 7**.

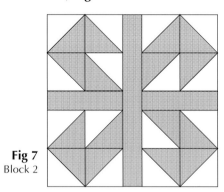

Fig 7
Block 2

Referring to **Fig 8**, join a Block 1 to two sides of a Template E square for row 1. Repeat for row 3. Then, join a Template E square to two sides of Block 2 for row 2. Join rows together.

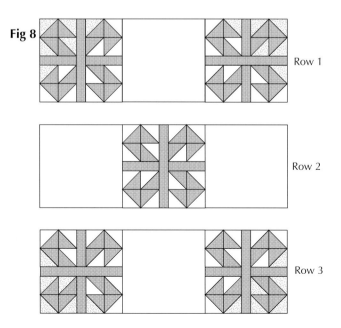

Fig 8

Row 1

Row 2

Row 3

Join a Unit B and a Unit C to each side of a Template B rectangle for Half Blocks, **Fig 9**. Repeat three more times.

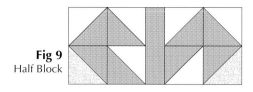

Fig 9
Half Block

Join a Template C triangle to Template D and Template D reversed pieces, **Fig 10**. Join these to Half Blocks to complete Border Units, **Fig 11**.

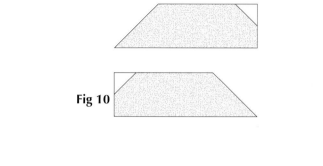

Fig 10

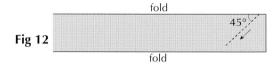

Fig 11 - Border Unit

Attach shorter side of each Border Unit to sides of quilt top stopping at dot. Sew diagonal seam to form miter in each corner.

Attach outer large floral print border, mitering corners.

To make ruched roses, fold long edges (wrong sides together) of 1" x 16" red strip to meet along the center of the back side. Strip will now be 1/2" x 16". With quilting thread to match fabric and starting on the upper right edge of strip, make running stitches diagonally at a 45° angle, **Fig 12**.

fold

45°

Fig 12

fold

When you reach lower edge of strip and needle is on top, bring needle over edge and up from the back; continue sewing running stitches at a 45° angle towards top of strip, **Fig 13**.

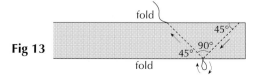

fold

45°

Fig 13

90°

45°

45°

fold

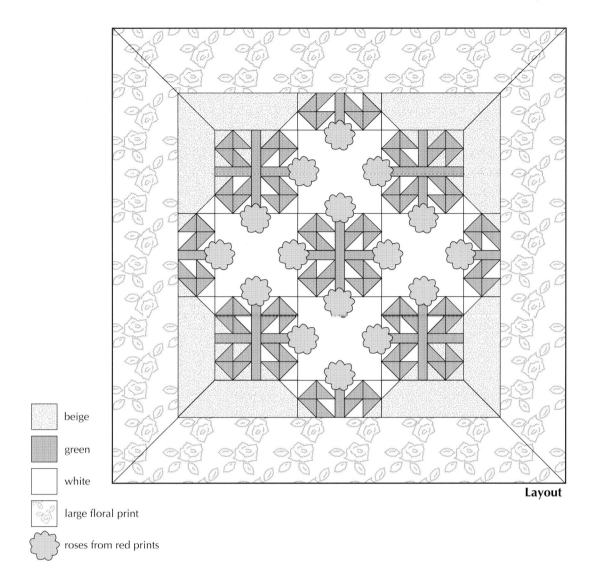

beige

green

white

large floral print

roses from red prints

Layout

Stitch in this manner for 4"; pull thread and arrange gathers. The edges of the ruching should have definite scallops, and should not be pulled too tightly, **Fig 14**. Continue stitching and gathering for entire length of strip.

Fig 14

Thread a second needle. Holding ruching in left hand, turn end around in a clockwise direction; tuck end under ruching and tack in place with second needle. Do not cut off thread.

Bring first petal up on top of ruching stitch line (the line that runs along the middle of the gathered strip), and stab stitch in place with second needle. Continue turning in

clockwise manner and tack each petal with stab stitch, **Fig 15**. Don't force petals to be in a certain place, let the edges follow the ruching stitch line.

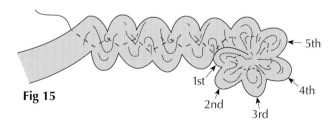

Fig 15

When rose is complete, tuck tail under flower and tack in place. Take a few stitches with first needle to secure.

Applique flowers as shown in layout using enough stitches to hold firmly in place.

Layer quilt with backing wrong side up, batting and finally, quilt with right side up. Quilt as desired; add binding.

19

(continued)

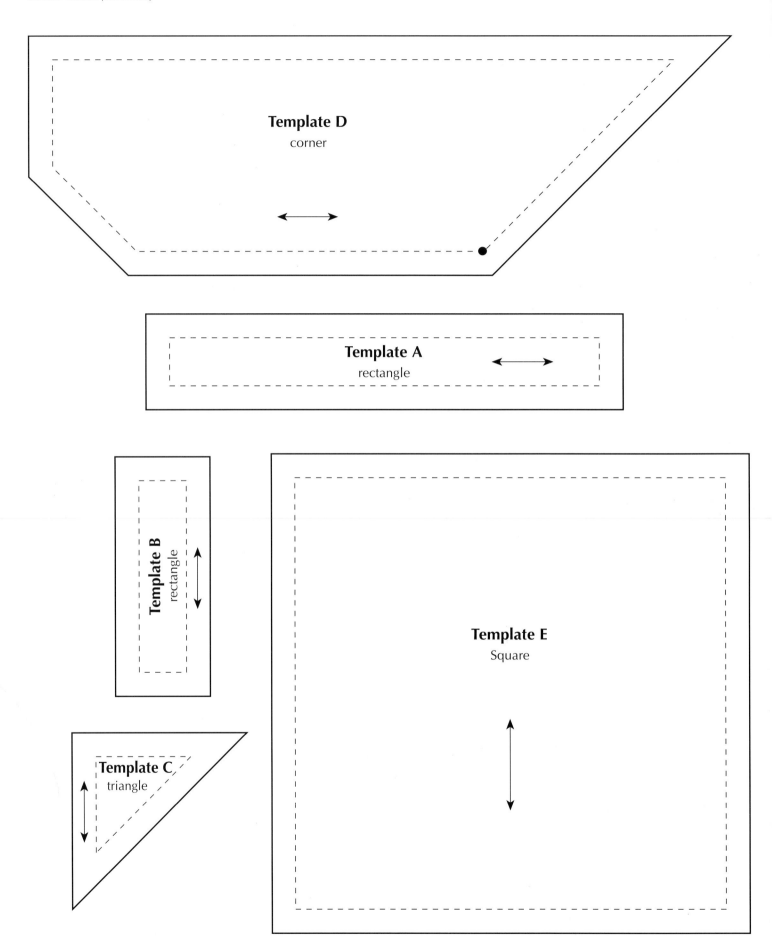

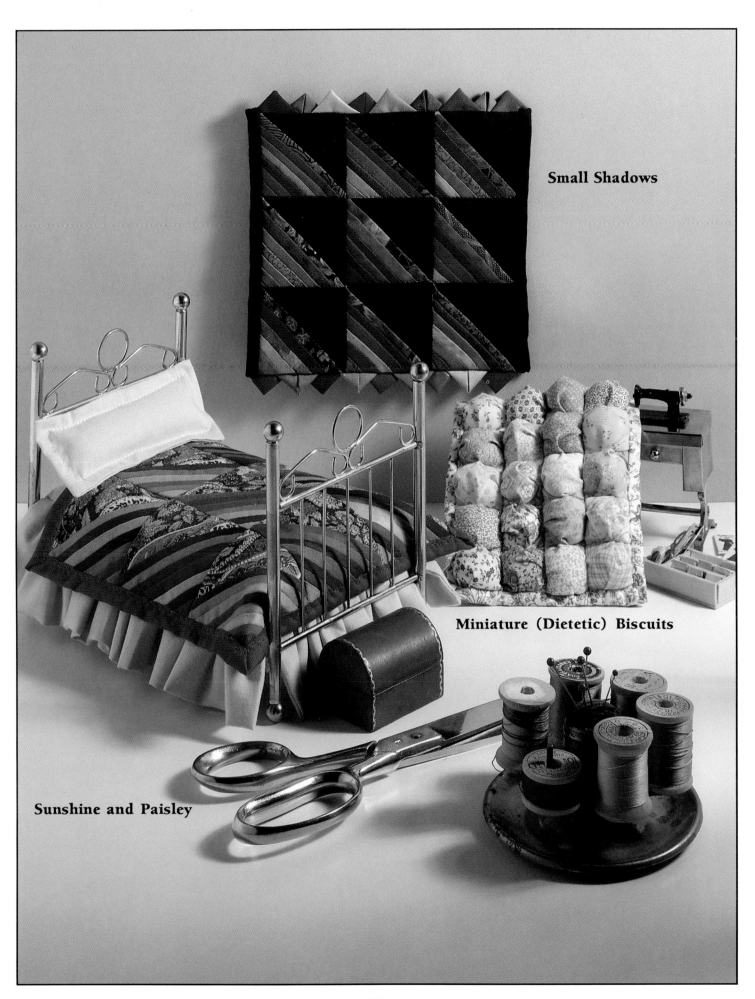

Small Shadows

Miniature (Dietetic) Biscuits

Sunshine and Paisley

21

Hearts of My Heart

Woven Roman Stripe

**String Star and Stripes -
Long May She Wave**

View Through the Attic Window at Fabrics From the '20s

When the Deep Purple Falls...

23

Starry, Starry Night

Log Cabin and Applique Hearts

Shown in color on front cover

APPROXIMATE SIZE: 15" x 18"

Donna McConnell is a real neat person, and all her quilting endeavors are really neat, too. Donna not only has a mail order business of patterns and kits, she travels and is much sought after by Quilt Guilds throughout the country. Her booth at the major quilt shows is always crowded and I truly feel it is a special privilege for her to share one of her lovely miniature quilts with us. I just know you will enjoy this treasured beauty.

FABRIC REQUIREMENTS:

six to eight assorted light print scraps
six to eight assorted dark print scraps
3/4" x 12" strip of rose solid
six assorted medium to dark print scraps (for hearts)
1/3 yd soft neutral print
fat quarter black solid
fat quarter burgundy solid
1/3 yd bright bold print
1/2 yd backing fabric
1/2 yd batting (Donna splits hers to achieve a thinner look for her miniatures.)

ADDITIONAL MATERIALS:

6" square of paper-backed fusible web
   (i.e. Wonder-Under™)

(continued)

TEMPLATES:

A background square
B side triangle
C corner triangle
D heart

CUTTING REQUIREMENTS:

3/4"-wide strips from assorted dark and light prints for
    Log Cabin Blocks
six Template A squares from soft neutral print for
    background squares
ten Template B side triangles from soft neutral print
four Template C corner triangles from soft neutral print
six Template D hearts from assorted medium to dark
    prints*
two 3/4" x 10 3/4" strips from black for inner border
two 3/4" x 8 3/4" strips from black for inner border
two 1 1/4" x 11 1/2" strips from burgundy for middle
    border
two 1 1/4" x 10 1/2" strips from burgundy for middle
    border
two 3" x 13" strips from large bold print for outer border
two 3" x 15" strips from large bold print for outer border
two 1 3/4" x 16" strips from large bold print for binding
two 1 3/4" x 19" strips from large bold print for binding
one 16" x 19" piece from backing fabric
*Read manufacturer's directions and press fusible web to
back of fabrics before cutting hearts.

INSTRUCTIONS:

Take a careful look at the Log Cabin Block diagram, **Fig 1**.
The block is divided diagonally into a dark half and a light
half with one single center square.

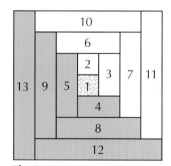

Fig 1 - Log Cabin Block

Place one light print fabric right sides together with solid
rose strip; stitch using 1/4" seam allowance. Press seam,
then cut twelve pieces at 3/4" intervals, **Fig 2**.

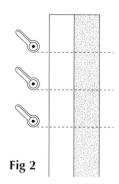

Fig 2

Place these pieced strips right sides together with a lt print
strip; stitch, **Fig 3;** press. Cut strip between pieced strip,
Fig 4. Place these sections on a dk print strip; stitch, cut,
and press, **Fig 5**. Add remaining strips in same manner,
referring to Log Cabin Block, **Fig 1**, for placement of lights
and darks. Set blocks aside.

Remove backing and fuse a heart to the center of each
background square. Applique heart edges by hand or with
a machine zigzag stitch.

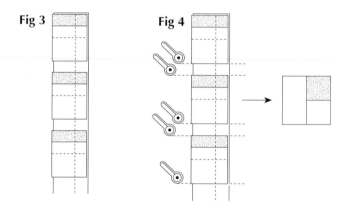

Fig 3   **Fig 4**

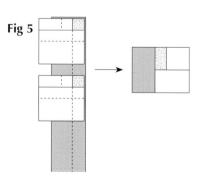

Fig 5

Following **Fig 6**, join Log Cabin and Heart blocks, adding side and corner triangles where necessary. **Note**: Be careful that all of your Log Cabin blocks have the same placement (all light halves pointing in the same direction).

After joining all your rows, press, and check that your quilt is square. Attach black inner border, sides first, then top and bottom. Attach middle and outer borders in same manner.

Layer quilt with backing wrong side up, then batting and quilt top right side up. Quilt as desired.

Fold binding strips in half lengthwise with wrong sides together and stitch to all four sides; turn to back of quilt and blind stitch in place.

Fig 6

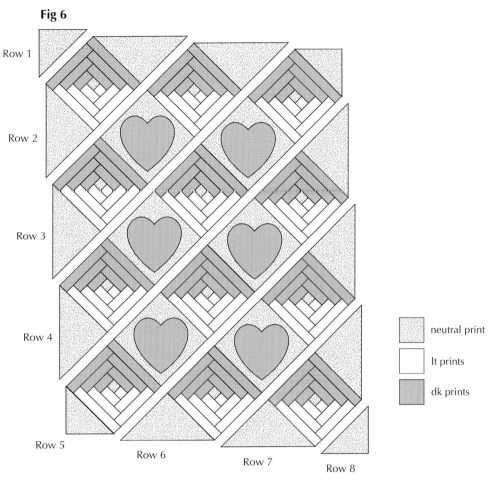

neutral print

lt prints

dk prints

Row 1
Row 2
Row 3
Row 4
Row 5
Row 6
Row 7
Row 8

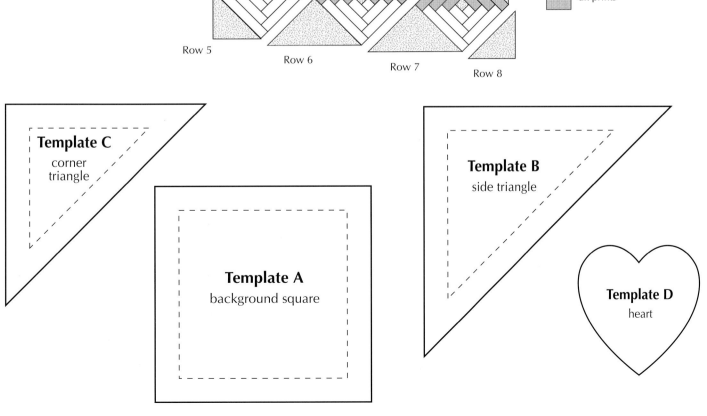

Template C
corner triangle

Template A
background square

Template B
side triangle

Template D
heart

27

Woven Roman Stripe

Shown in color on page 22

APPROXIMATE SIZE: 11" x 16 1/2"

What better way to enjoy two fabrics that are reverse designs! This mini quilt uses the same print in two different combinations: black on beige and beige on black. There is a zing of red, both in the narrow border flap and red floss used for tying the quilt. This quilt will be one of your favorites and, yes, a real quickie as well.

FABRIC REQUIREMENTS:

1/2 yd black print
one fat quarter beige print
one fat quarter red
12" x 18" piece of batting or fleece

ADDITIONAL MATERIALS:

red embroidery floss

CUTTING REQUIREMENTS:

twelve 1 1/4" x 18" strips from black print
six 1 1/4" x 18" strips from beige print
two 1 1/2" x 12" strips from black print for border
two 1 1/4" x 18" strips from black print for border
two 1" x 12" strips from red
two 1" x 18" strips from red
one 12" x 18" piece for backing

INSTRUCTIONS:

Using 1/4" seams, stitch a black print strip on each side of a beige print strip, **Fig 1**. Press seams toward darker fabric using caution not to stretch. Make six sets.

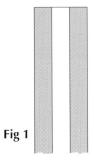

Fig 1

Cut rows at 2 3/4" intervals using caution not to stretch. You will need a total of forty blocks.

Join blocks alternating their direction, **Fig 2**. Measure and square up all sides.

Fig 2

For small flap borders, fold red strips in half lengthwise with wrong sides together; press. Place an 18" long red strip on each side of quilt top, raw edges even; baste. Place 12" long red strips along top and bottom edges of quilt, folding back ends so fold is even with fold on side strips, **Fig 3**; baste. Attach borders, sides first, then top and bottom, mitering corners if desired.

Add backing, then tie quilt at corner of each block with twelve strands of red embroidery floss.

Fig 3

Small Shadows

Shown in color on page 21

APPROXIMATE SIZE: 6 1/4" x 6 3/4"

Included in my previous book, "Reversible Quilts", is an Amish Sunshine and Shadow quilt using the same fabrics as in this mini quilt. Small Shadows was made from the leftover ends of the 1 1/2" strips used in the Amish Sunshine and Shadow reversible quilt. I simply cut the strips in half, giving me the 3/4" wide strips needed for this mini. It pays to never throw any of your small snippets away. Take a large safety pin, skewer them on it, and save them for the fun of making mini quilts of different sizes and patterns.

FABRIC REQUIREMENTS:

one fat quarter solid black
assorted scraps of prints and jewel tones
8" square of fleece or batting

TEMPLATES:

A 2 1/2" square
B 1 1/2" square

CUTTING REQUIREMENTS:

3/4"-wide strips for piecing
nine 2 1/2" squares from black for blocks
eighteen 1 1/2" squares from jewel tones for prairie
    points
two 1 1/4" x 8" strips from black for prairie point
    binding
two 2 3/4" x 8" strips from black for binding
one 8" x 8" piece from black for backing

INSTRUCTIONS:

Hint: I have found that using a zipper foot positioned to the right of the sewing machine needle is a fantastic way to keep your seams straight on such small pieces.

Draw diagonal line from corner to corner on a 2 1/2" black square; make a dashed line 1/4" from drawn line, **Fig 1**. Place raw edge of a 3/4"-wide strip along dashed line; stitch using 1/4" seam allowance, **Fig 2**. This first strip is now centered diagonally on block.

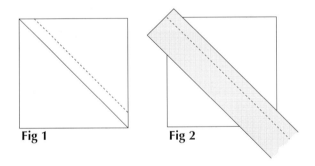

| Fig 1 | Fig 2 |

Fold strip over seam allowance, finger press in place, then trim strip even with square, **Fig 3**.

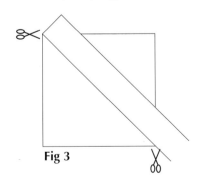

Fig 3

Add second strip right side down over first strip, matching raw edges; stitch using 1/4" seam allowance, **Fig 4**. Fold strip over seam allowance, press and trim. Continue in same manner until entire half of square is covered, **Fig 5**. You will use seven assorted strips for each block. Repeat for remaining eight blocks.

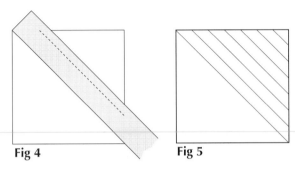

| Fig 4 | Fig 5 |

Arrange blocks as in photograph. Attach road maps (page 6); join blocks using 1/4" seam allowance.

Layer quilt with backing wrong side up, then batting and quilt top right side up. Quilt as desired.

Attach prairie points (page 5) to top and bottom of quilt. Attach binding to sides.

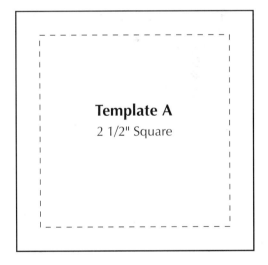

Template A
2 1/2" Square

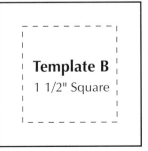

Template B
1 1/2" Square

Starry, Starry Night

Shown in color on page 24

APPROXIMATE SIZE: 18" x 28"

Dori Hawks is Executive Director of the American International Quilt Association as well as a very active member of the Quilt Guild of Greater Houston, the Contemporary Quilt Group, and the Wearable Arts group in Houston. The contemporary quilt she is sharing with us, was the one she made and donated to the Celebrity Auction held during The Quilt Festival in Houston in 1991. However, we must also thank June Bronson, as this lovely quilt is now from her collection.

FABRIC REQUIREMENTS:

5/8 yd dark blue fabric (photographed quilt used a hand-dyed fabric)

thirty-one 4" x 4" squares of assorted fabrics including metallics for stars

5/8 yd of backing fabric

1/2 yd silver metallic fabric for binding

18 1/2" x 28 1/2" piece of batting or fleece

ADDITIONAL MATERIALS:
metallic silver sewing thread
1/4 yd paper-backed fusible web
   (i.e. Wonder-Under™)
size 14 sewing machine needle

TEMPLATES:
A, B, C, and D for four sizes of stars

CUTTING REQUIREMENTS:
one 18 1/2" x 28 1/2" piece from dark blue for
   background
one 18 1/2" x 28 1/2" piece from backing fabric
3 yds of 1 3/4"-wide strips from metallic fabric
   for binding

INSTRUCTIONS:

Following manufacturer's directions, press fusible web to the back of all the 4" x 4" squares. Cut out stars using assorted star templates as follows: five of A; eighteen of B; six of C; and 2 of D. Remove paper from back of stars and place on background to create the effect of stars floating in the night sky; press in place.

Using the star templates and referring to photograph, mark quilting lines randomly across the background fabric as desired. Baste background fabric to your batting and backing. Using metallic thread and a size 14 sewing machine needle, machine stitch the stars onto your basted wall quilt. Dori says to be free with the stitching of the stars. In other words, you don't have to stay right on the lines and tips of the stars. Then quilt along your marked stars.

Attach silver metallic binding.

Stand back and watch your stars dancing through the night!

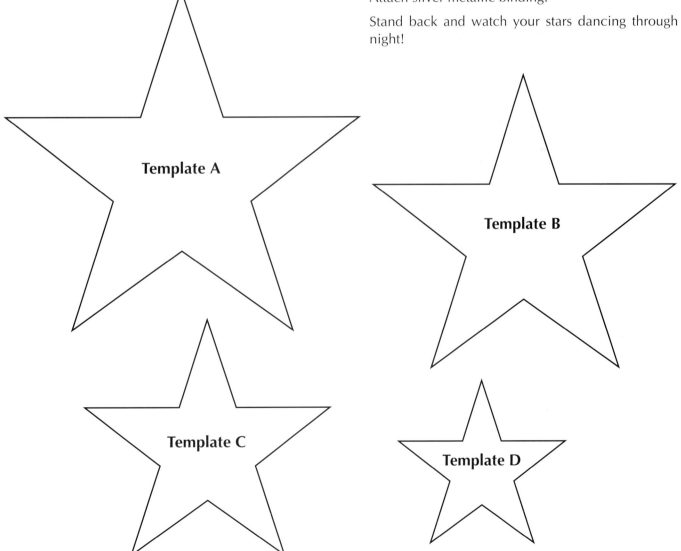

Template A

Template B

Template C

Template D

Postage Stamp Doll Bed Quilt

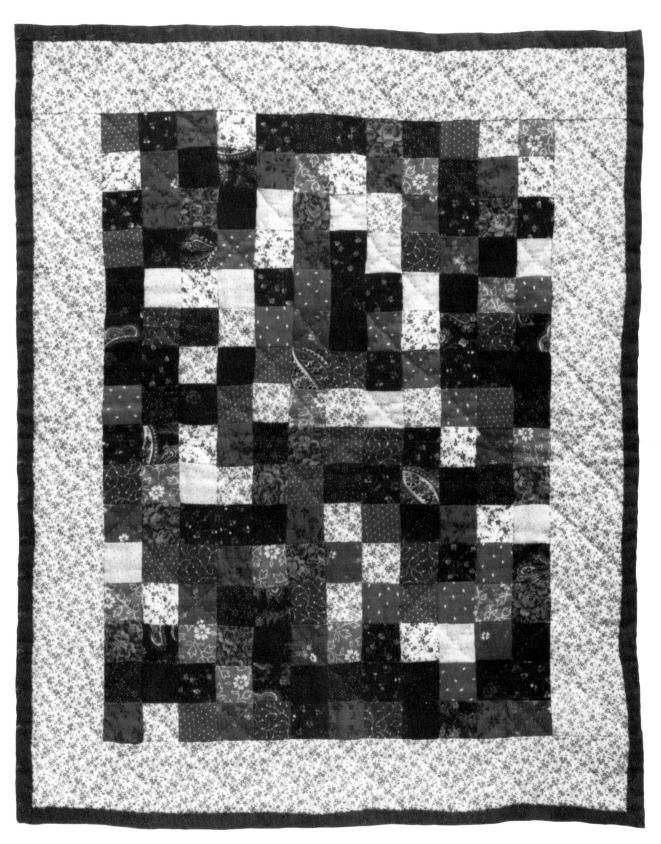

Shown in color on back cover

APPROXIMATE SIZE: 15 1/2" x 19 1/2"

I first met Kim De Coste while taking a Seminole Piecing class from Lassie Whittman in 1979 at the Quilt Patch in Houston, Texas. He made this dear doll bed quilt after seeing a similar quilt in an antique magazine. He chose fabrics as close to the ones of yesteryear as he could find. I am truly proud to own one of his "creations".

FABRIC REQUIREMENTS:

sixteen assorted fat quarters
one fat quarter for border
one fat quarter for backing/binding
18" x 22" piece of batting

CUTTING REQUIREMENTS:

sixteen 1 1/2" x 18" strips from assorted colors
four 2 1/2" x 16 1/2" strips for border

INSTRUCTIONS:

Sew four strips together lengthwise; cut at 1 1/2" intervals, **Fig 1**. Repeat with remaining strips. You will have a total of forty-eight pieced strips.

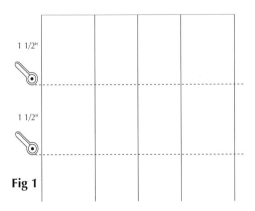

Fig 1

Sew four strips together randomly to form a block of sixteen small squares, **Fig 2**. Repeat for a total of twelve 16-patch blocks.

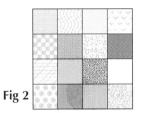

Fig 2

Sew the 16-patch blocks together as in layout, turning blocks in different directions to give a completely random effect.

Layout

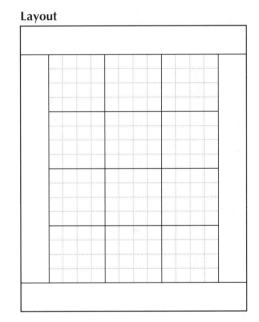

Add border to sides first, then top and bottom.

Cut backing the size of your quilt top plus 1/2" on all four sides; place wrong side up. Center batting, then quilt top right side up on top of backing. Quilt as desired. Fold in edges of backing and bring to front; blind stitch in place.

View Through the Attic Window
at Fabrics from the '20s

*Shown in color
on page 23*

APPROXIMATE SIZE: 12 1/2" x 17"

Quilts are markers in women's lives. The fabrics used in the quilts are clues to the approximate year in which they were made. The fabrics in this special doll bed quilt are fun prints of the early '20s when there was a surge of interest in children's prints. You will see many different designs while peaking through the mini attic window. Attic Window is a favorite pattern in any size you choose to make it, and it enhances a collection of special fabrics. My special thanks to Meredith Rials of Lake Charles, Louisiana who shared so many of these prints with me.

FABRIC REQUIREMENTS:

sixteen assorted print scraps
one fat quarter dk turquoise
one fat quarter lt turquoise
1/2 yd black
one 15" x 20" piece of batting or fleece

TEMPLATES:

A window
B left window frame
C bottom window frame

CUTTING REQUIREMENTS:

sixteen Template A from assorted prints for windows

sixteen Template B from dk turquoise for left window frames*

sixteen Template C from lt turquoise for bottom window frames*

one 1 1/4" x 15 1/2" strip from dk turquoise for right side of windows

one 1 1/4" x 11" strip from dk turquoise for top of windows

two 1 3/4" x 13 1/2" strips from black for border

two 1 3/4" x 18" strips from black for border

two 9 1/2" x 13" pieces from black for backing

***Note**: Transfer the dot marking onto each Template B and Template C piece.

INSTRUCTIONS:

Stitch dk turquoise Template B window frame to the left side of Template A window stopping at dot, **Fig 1**. Add the lt turquoise Template C window frame at the bottom of window to dot, **Fig 2**; press. Sew diagonal edges of Templates B and C to dot, **Fig 3**. Repeat for a total of 16 blocks.

Pin blocks up to check fabric placement; attach road maps (page 6); then join blocks.

Attach dk turquoise strips to top and right sides, mitering upper right corner if desired.

Attach black borders sides first, then top and bottom, mitering corners if desired.

Refer to Pillowcase Method 2 (page 7) to finish quilt. Quilt as desired.

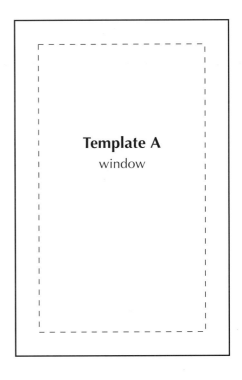

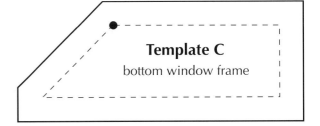

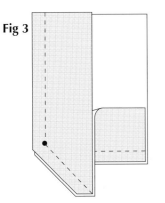

School House –
Where It All Begins!

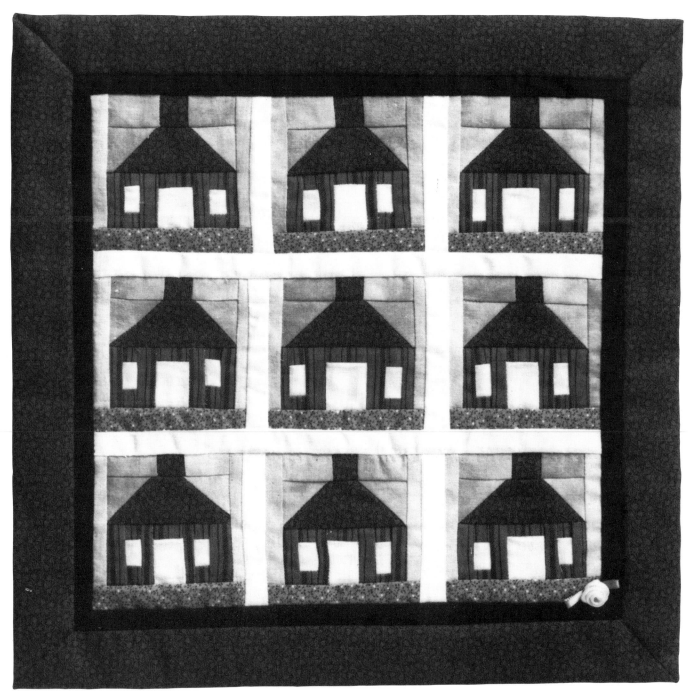

Shown in color on front cover

APPROXIMATE SIZE: 11" x 11"

What happy memories are evoked by the School House pattern! This mini School House quilt was made in honor of all our wonderful teachers, including my three daughters. Thanks for those "good old golden rule" days.

FABRIC REQUIREMENTS:

one fat quarter tie-dyed blue
1/2 yd red print
one fat quarter red stripe
one fat quarter white
1/8 yd green print
1/8 yd black
11" square of fleece or batting

CUTTING REQUIREMENTS:

one 1" x 10" strip from red print for bell tower

two 1 1/4" x 10" strips from blue for sky

one 2 1/2" x 13" strip from red print for roof top

two 1 1/4" x 13" strips from blue for sky

two 3/4" x 15" strips from red stripe (cut crosswise)
    for top and bottom of window

four 3/4" x 15" strips from red stripe (cut lengthwise)
    for sides of window

one 1" x 15" strip from white for windows

one 3/4" x 10" strip from red stripe (cut crosswise)
    for top of door

one 1" x 1 1/4" strip from white for door

three 3/4" x 18" strips from blue for sky

two 1" x 18" strips from green print for grass

six 1" x 3" strips from white for sashing

three 1" x 9" strips from white for sashing

four 1" x 10" strips from black for first border

one 14" x 14" square from red print for backing
    and border

INSTRUCTIONS:

Note: Sew 1/4" seams, then trim seam allowance to 1/8" after each step.

Sew blue 1 1/4" x 10" strip to each side of 1" x 10" red print strip; press, then cut at 1" intervals for nine Bell Tower Units, **Fig 1**. Set aside. **Hint:** These little pieces are much easier to keep track of if you place them on a 12" x 12" piece of fleece. The fleece also makes it easier to transfer small pieces from cutting area to your sewing machine since fabric tends to stick to the fleece.

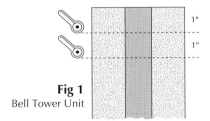

Fig 1
Bell Tower Unit

Cut 2 1/2" x 13" red print strip into nine 1 1/4" pieces. Cut 1 1/4" x 13" blue strips into eighteen 1 1/4" squares. Place a blue square right sides together on each side of 2 1/2" x 1 1/4" red print piece. Attach each square by starting at corner, sewing diagonally towards center, turning and

going back down diagonally through other square, **Fig 2**. Press blue back onto itself, **Fig 3**. It is not necessary to cut the red or under side of the blue triangles away, as it seems to add a bit of stability. You need nine Roof Units.

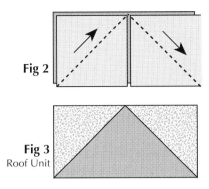

Fig 2

Fig 3
Roof Unit

Join Bell Tower Unit to top edge of Roof Unit, making sure tower matches rooftop, **Fig 4**. Press and set aside.

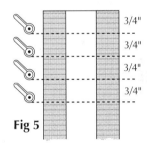

Fig 4

Sew a 3/4" x 15" crosswise red stripe piece to each side of the 1" x 15" white strip for window; press seams toward red, then cut eighteen pieces at 3/4" intervals, **Fig 5,** for window pieces.

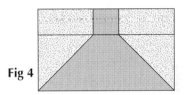

3/4"

3/4"

3/4"

3/4"

Fig 5

Place window piece right sides together on a 3/4" x 15" lengthwise red stripe strip; stitch. Continue chain piecing, **Fig 6**, until all eighteen window pieces are sewn; press. Cut red strip between window pieces, then repeat for other side of window piece to complete eighteen Window Units, **Fig 7**.

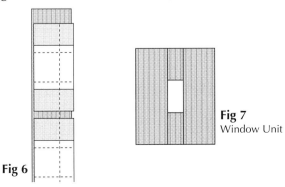

Fig 6

Fig 7
Window Unit

(continued)

Sew 3/4" x 10" red stripe strip to 1 1/4" x 10" white strip; press towards red. Cut at 1" intervals for nine Door Units, **Fig 8**.

Fig 8
Door Unit

Sew a Window Unit to each side of Door Unit; continue chain piecing until nine Building Units are completed, **Fig 9**; press.

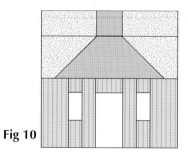

Fig 9
Building Unit

Join Building Unit to Roof/Bell Tower Unit; chain piece until you have nine School Houses, **Fig 10**.

Fig 10

Place School House right side down on 3/4" x 18" blue strip; stitch. Continue chain piecing, then cut blue strip between School Houses. Repeat for other side of School Houses, **Fig 11**; press.

Fig 11

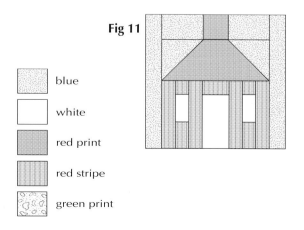

- blue
- white
- red print
- red stripe
- green print

Place bottom edge of School House along 1" x 18" green strip with right sides together; stitch. Continue chain piecing until you have completed nine School House Blocks, **Fig 12**.

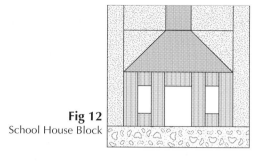

Fig 12
School House Block

Join blocks into three rows with 1" x 3" white sashing strips in between blocks, **Fig 13**; press.

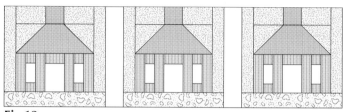

Fig 13

Join rows using 1" x 9" white sashing strips between rows, **Fig 14**; press.

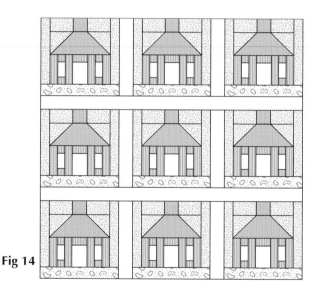

Fig 14

Attach black border, sides first, then top and bottom, mitering corners if desired.

Cut batting 1" larger than the size of quilt top on all four sides, approximately 10 1/2" x 10 1/2". Place backing wrong side up, then center batting and quilt top right side up. Bring edges of backing toward front and blind stitch to black border, forming a 1" border all around.

Sunshine and Paisley

Shown in color on page 21

APPROXIMATE SIZE: 6 1/2" x 6 1/2"

Sunshine and Paisley is made the same way as Small Shadows, only the placement of the solids and prints is reversed. Some quilters are afraid that too busy a print will not give as effective and striking an effect as when the predominate areas use a solid. But hopefully this little dear will help you to visualize other tones, other movement.

FABRIC REQUIREMENTS:

1 fat quarter raspberry solid
1 fat quarter paisley print
twelve assorted solids (scraps)
7" square of batting or fleece

TEMPLATES:

A square

CUTTING REQUIREMENTS:

nine 2 1/2" squares from paisley for blocks
3/4"-wide strips from assorted solids for piecing
one 7 1/2" x 7 1/2" piece from raspberry fabric
   for backing

INSTRUCTIONS:

Make nine blocks following instructions for Small Shadows on page 30. **Note:** You may use 1/4" masking tape to mark stitching lines if your marking pencil doesn't show up well on a print.

Place blocks as in layout, attach road maps (page 6) and join using 1/4" seam allowances.

Layer backing wrong side up, then batting and quilt top right side up. Backing should extend 1/2" on all four sides. Quilt as desired. Fold in edges of backing and bring to front; stitch in place.

Layout

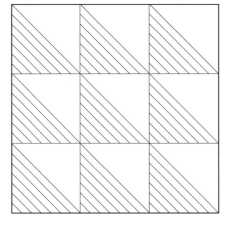

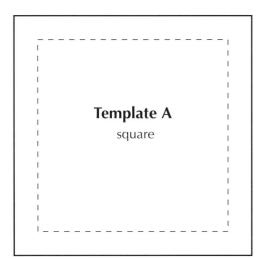

Template A
square

41

String Star & Stripes –
Long May She Wave

Shown in color on page 22

APPROXIMATE SIZE: 12 1/2" x 13 1/2"

Quilters of years past truly lived by the saying, "Make do or do without". Therefore, every lady had a poke bag or old pillowcase where she put "strings" or strips of fabric to save for string piecing. A "string" is any piece of fabric that is longer than it is wide. You can collect "strings" from the leveling of a hem for a skirt, from the trimming off of extra fabrics, and from the squaring up of your quilt blocks.

Many quilt patterns are string pieced (i.e. Tulip, Spider Web, and Carolina Lily just to name a few). My favorite string-pieced pattern is the Star String pattern. You can make this block from 7" (the size I am using in my flag) to 17" (the size so often given in quilt books). If you don't have a bag full of strings, try my quick method of string piecing and before you know it, you'll have your own personal quilted FLAG!

FABRIC REQUIREMENTS:
one fat quarter red
one fat quarter white
1/4 yd navy blue
nine strips of red/white prints (minimum 18" long)
one fat quarter print for backing
14" x 15" piece of batting or fleece

TEMPLATES:
A diamond without seam allowance
A diamond with seam allowance
B background square for star
C background triangle for star

CUTTING REQUIREMENTS:
six 1" x 18" strips from assorted red prints
three 3/4" x 18" strips from assorted red prints
four squares from navy blue
four triangles from navy blue
four 1 1/2" x 7 1/2" strips from red
three 1 1/2" x 7 1/2" strips from white
three 1 1/2" x 15 1/2" from white
three 1 1/2" x 15 1/2" strips from red
one 13" x 14" piece from backing fabric

INSTRUCTIONS:

Sew nine 18" long strips together lengthwise to create a fabric that measures 4 1/4" x 18"; press. Using Template A diamond with seam allowance, draw eight diamonds on string-pieced fabric, **Fig 1**. Using Template A diamond without seam allowance, draw 1/4" seam allowances and mark dots inside each diamond.

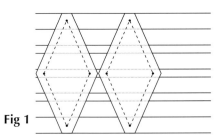

Fig 1

With right sides together and matching the drawn stitching lines, stitch diamonds together from the tip toward the elbow, **Fig 2**. STOP SEWING AT THE DOT AND BACKSTITCH A FEW STITCHES. Continue until all diamonds are sewn together.

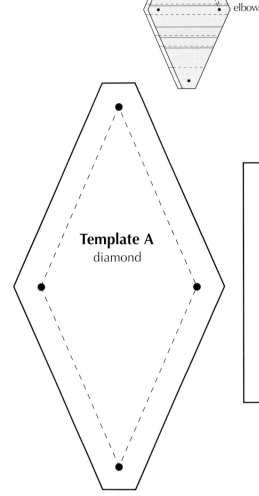

Fig 2

tip

elbow

Attach squares and triangles in same manner, starting from the outer tip and stitching to the elbow dot. Do not stitch the seam allowance down or star will not lay flat. Square off your Star Block, **Fig 3**.

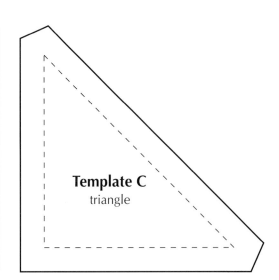

Fig 3
Star Block

Sew 1 1/2" x 7 1/2" red and white strips together, starting and ending with a red strip; press seams toward red strips. Stitch to one side of the star for upper half of flag.

Sew remaining 15 1/2" red and white strips together and join to upper half of flag, making sure that red strip is at the bottom.

With quilt top and backing right sides together, and your fleece on the bottom, stitch together using Pillowcase Method 1 (page 6); trim edges and turn right sides out. Machine or hand quilt around the outline of the star, then quilt wavy lines in the stripes to give a windblown quilting look.

Enjoy your quilt and the freedom that the flag symbolizes.

Template A
diamond

Template B
square

Template C
triangle

When the Deep Purple Falls

APPROXIMATE SIZE: 6 1/2" x 15 1/2"

Remember when you were given an English assignment to finish an essay in 30 minutes? Well, this mini wall quilt was a class assignment for a workshop given by Nancy Halpern. We had to express an idea in an hour with the fabrics we had on hand. My fabrics reminded me of the colors of the sky at different times of the day — the blue represented dawn; the gold, high noon; the rust, sunset; and the purple, that lovely song of the '50s, "When the Deep Purple Falls". Find one little corner that looks small and bare and add the joy of this miniature wall quilt.

FABRIC REQUIREMENTS:

one fat quarter of black
1/8 yd each of four solids, (i.e. blue, gold, rust, purple)
1/8 yd each of four striped fabrics to complement solids
6 1/2" x 15 1/2" piece of batting

TEMPLATES:

A square
B corner

CUTTING REQUIREMENTS:

one Template A square from each solid
one Template B corner from each striped fabric*
one Template B corner reversed from each
   striped fabric*
10 1/2" x 19 1/2" rectangle from black for backing
***Note**: Transfer the dot marking onto each
   Template B piece.

Shown in color on page 23